27 Messages
of
Comfort
from
Heaven

Matthew Robert Payne

27 Messages of Comfort from Heaven

Matthew Robert Payne

RWG Publishing

Please visit http://personal-prophecy-today.com to sow into Matthew's writing ministry to request a personal prophecy or other prophetic services.

GET YOUR FREE BOOKS BY MATTHEW ROBERT PAYNE

To read more than 40 of Matthew Robert Payne's books for free, please visit https://matthewrobertpayne.com.

Matthew also has 87 books in total on Amazon Kindle for 99 cents. You can find them here https://tinyurl.com/p69rch5x

Cover Designed by Akira007 on Fiverr.com

Dedication

This book is written for and dedicated to the people pursuing God and everything He has for them. This collection of personal prophetic words are for me, but it is my prayer you will be comforted by the messages.

Introduction

————

A re you feeling defeated and overcome by sinful habits and need some personal renewal? Matthew was suffering from sleep issues, demonic problems and sex addiction that just would not quit. Overcome from his suffering, he was in search of a fresh now word from God and that is when his scribe angel Bethany inspired him to write this book.

After listening to her inspiration Matthew went on to record 27 videos of prophetic words from twenty saints from heaven, three angels, Jesus the Father and his mother and father. What followed was an over fifty-page book full of encouraging prophetic words that gave him comfort and putt him in another state of mind with feelings that he would one day overcome.

This is a deeply personal book that enriched his life and promises to give you insight into just how well the people of heaven can impact your life if you have ears to hear from them.

Chapter 1 Moses

———

I am writing to offer you encouragement and support in your journey towards healing and freedom from addiction. I understand that you have been struggling for over 40 years, seeking comfort in the arms of strange women, but finding no peace or release.

It's important to remember that God is with you and loves you deeply. He delights in you and sees you as precious. Despite the difficulties you face, there is hope. You have experienced freedom from your addiction three times in the past 10 years, and I believe that it will happen again.

The key to your deliverance is to seek the help of the Holy Spirit and to wait for His grace. Be vigilant in your relationship with the Lord Jesus, the Father, and the Holy Spirit. Work on building intimacy with them and continue to be transparent and honest in all that you do and say.

I know that the road ahead may seem difficult and insurmountable, but I have faith that you will overcome this challenge and find peace. Keep fighting the good fight and remember that God is always by your side.

Chapter 2 Joshua

———

Dear Matthew,

I hope this message finds you well. I wanted to take the opportunity to reach out and share some encouragement with you regarding your struggles. As someone who grew up under the mentorship of Moses and witnessed the wonders of God's power and love, I can attest to the fact that you serve a faithful and loving God.

Through reading the stories in the Bible, you will see time and time again that God is faithful to those who trust in him. That is why I encourage you to place your trust in the Holy Spirit and in God's ability to heal you from any struggles you may be facing, whether it be addiction, sleep issues, or mental illness.

You serve a God who has performed impossible feats and defeated impossible battles in the past. And just as God was with us in the past, he will also be with you in your future. You have the favor of God in your life and he will not leave you defeated or in bondage.

God is a healer and he is full of love, compassion, and kindness. He is slow to anger and forgiving to the utmost degree. So, be confident that the same God who led us to victory in the promised land will also lead you to victory in your future.

It was an honor to speak with you today and I hope this message brings you comfort and encouragement.

Chapter 3 Elijah

———

Dear friend, I want to share my thoughts on the topic of feeling like giving up on life. I understand the struggle and pain of wanting to leave this world behind. I personally experienced this myself when I was facing challenges and attacks from Jezebel. However, I want to encourage you that there is hope and peace to be found through a relationship with God.

Drawing close to God in intimacy and building a real relationship with him will provide a safe haven and help ease the thoughts of wanting to escape this world. Many people reading this message may feel the same way, but I want to assure you that there is a brighter future ahead.

I lived through this feeling of despair, but God ultimately answered my prayer and took me away. However, as written in Revelation Chapter 11, I will come back to earth and serve as a prophet. It will be a difficult task, but God has a purpose for us all and has not called us to an easy life.

Matthew, I know you have faced your own battles with the Jezebel spirit and have struggled with seeking deliverance. But I want to remind you of God's faithfulness and love for you. He delivers and heals his servants, and they prosper and see success in the land of the living. You have been called as a prophet and have the power to speak life into others and bring encouragement and education to those around you.

Remember, you are a true friend of God and he holds a special place in his heart for you. You will overcome the Jezebel spirit and experience victory in your personal life. Be confident in your abilities and trust in God's love and guidance.

Chapter 4 Enoch

———

The book of Enoch has been generating much buzz lately and many readers are drawn to its accounts. I want to express my belief that the book is authentic and trustworthy. Despite its seemingly unconventional nature, reading it twice will give you a deeper understanding of its content.

What I really want to discuss with you, Matthew, is the importance of having a close and intimate relationship with Jesus, God the Father, the Holy Spirit, and the saints in heaven. Regardless of any addictions, mental health struggles, traumatic experiences, or even instances of demonic possession, it's crucial to remain close to God. Cultivate a daily dialogue with him and aim to understand his heart and the heart of Jesus. The ultimate goal is to embody Jesus' character and share it with others.

I have experienced a profound and intimate connection with God, often being taken up to heaven and spending time with him. The glory of heaven is so magnificent that it's hard to return to the earthly realm. At times, heaven sends people to you as a sign of your close relationship with God. Despite being referred to as God's Enoch, you have a mission to fulfill on Earth and many books to write and Christians to educate and encourage on behalf of God.

I encourage you to continue seeking a deeper understanding of God and Jesus. Ask more questions, delve into their hearts, and obey Jesus as your master. The Holy Spirit plays a crucial role in leading your life, and I commend you for your close friendship with God. We are proud of you and I am personally proud of you as well.

Chapter 5 Joseph The Dreamer

———

Hello, Matthew, it's great to be speaking with you. You had a vision of heaven many years ago and during that visit, Jesus placed a coat of many colors on you. You cherished this coat and it has been a source of comfort for you, especially during the years when you felt trapped in a prison due to your struggles with addiction.

I am proud to say that even while you were in this difficult place, you utilized your gift of prophecy, and I discuss how I used my gift in prison also, in an interview with me that was published in a book.

You can get that book here https://tinyurl.com/54929fux

You continue to use your gifts while still in the prison, undiscovered by the wider Christian community and without a large platform. Despite this, you offer personal prophecies to people on the streets of Sydney, Australia, encouraging and lifting them up. You run a prophetic website, where people can receive a prophecy in exchange for a donation. Your actions show that Jesus speaks through you, as you've inspired and encouraged so many people.

You draw strength from the coat of many colors and continue to use your gifts while still in the prison. You've even been writing books while there, and I commend you for keeping yourself busy.

Stay encouraged, there will come a day when you will be discovered, gain more popularity, and no longer suffer.

Chapter 6 Joseph Jesus' father

———

Greetings, Matthew, it's a great honor to connect with you. As a parent, I have experienced the joy of raising a son who was guided by the Holy Spirit from a young age. He lived a life of obedience, never straying from the path set before him and always doing what was right.

I have kept an eye on your life and I am aware of your struggles, including your addiction to the sex industry. Despite this challenge, I can see that you are deeply committed to following the leadings of the Holy Spirit and your obedience is evident in the majority of your life.

From my vantage point in heaven, I have watched my son's entire life unfold, and I was struck by his joy, kindness, and the way he lifted up and encouraged those around him. I know that you too, despite times of sadness and suffering, including your mental illness and addiction, remain a source of encouragement and positivity for those around you.

You are truly a reflection of Jesus, who also faced difficult times, but never let his struggles dim his light. He was always there to lift people up, and you carry on this legacy by spreading joy, giving compliments, and positively impacting the lives of those you encounter.

I want to encourage you to keep trusting, keep serving, and remember that you serve a faithful God who will never abandon you. You will emerge from your trials and suffering into a place of recognition, safety, blessing, and prosperity. May the light of Jesus always shine upon you and bless you.

Chapter 7 Mary, Jesus' mother

———

Greetings, Matthew! It is a true honor to have this opportunity to speak with you. I recently had the privilege of spending some quality time with your dear mother who is now in heaven. During our time together, we spoke of you and the challenges you are facing in life. Your mother is aware of the difficulties you face, including your addiction, mental health struggles, and sleep issues, but she is at peace in heaven, where worries and concerns are left behind. She has even seen visions of your future and is overjoyed at what she sees.

Your mother's happiness is well-deserved, as you have accomplished so much in your life, Matthew. In just a couple of weeks, you will reach a major milestone by publishing your 100th book. Your writing is inspiring and has touched many people's lives. Despite the fact that some of your books may contain typos, those who read them are able to understand the message and connect with the love and compassion that you pour into each word. Your character is truly remarkable, and I am impressed by your demonstration of the love and kindness of Jesus in your daily life.

Just yesterday, for example, you encountered a homeless man sitting at a bus stop, looking dishevelled and in need. Your kindness and compassion shone through as you gave him $50, and when he was overcome with tears, you went a step further and gave him an additional $60. This is a testament to your amazing character and the way you live your life guided by the Spirit of God.

In heaven, there are many who know your name and delight in your life and accomplishments. You are a true son of God, and heaven is proud of you. In fact, 27 people in heaven have spoken to you through your book, and if you were to know more characters from the Bible, there could have been 100 or more! You are an overcomer, and deliverance and healing will come for you.

Although you may not be accepted by all Christians, you will always be loved by the simple people and those who have experienced life's difficulties. You will continue to minister to others and bring hope and comfort to those who need it. It was a genuine pleasure speaking with you today, and I hope that my words have encouraged and uplifted you.

Chapter 8 Mary Magdalene

———

Dear Matthew, we have been together through many moments in your life and have had many adventures together. For those who may not understand, I have the ability to bilocate, which means I exist in both heaven and on earth simultaneously. I frequently accompany you on your trips to the shopping center, and I am always by your side when you leave your home. I often communicate with you when I am with you, letting you know that I am there for you.

Yesterday, I was with you when you generously gave that man $110. I used my influence on you, instead of the Holy Spirit, to inspire you to give him the money. I spoke to you through the voice of the Holy Spirit, encouraging and blessing you as you made the gift.

Matthew, you are truly a blessing to those around you. You possess many of the same qualities as the Jesus I walked with during his time on earth. He was always interacting with people, saying hello, lifting their spirits, and showering them with compliments, miracles, and blessings. Although you have not yet performed any physical healings, I believe that will change in the future. You are a person of joy and positivity, and it brings me great joy to be with you.

I am always with you, even during the difficult times when you suffer from sleep issues or are struggling with mental illness. I understand the personal trauma and unhealed wounds in your life and I love you deeply. Our relationship has grown stronger through our many encounters, and I am proud and happy to be a part of your life.

I have seen your future, and I know that you will be a powerful overcomer.

You serve a faithful and loving God who can heal you, set you free, deliver you from your struggles, and bring you recognition and respect within the Christian community. Your life will resemble that of Joseph, who was once bound and in prison but went on to rescue Egypt and its people, performing mighty miracles along the way. The best is yet to come, and it is an honor to be a part of this book of encouragement from heaven. Heaven is rooting for you and this book is one of their favorites. I could go on and on, sharing so much more with you, but for now, I will cut this short and simply say that I am here for you and always cheering you on.

Chapter 9 Mary of Bethany

———

Hi Matthew, it's great to have this conversation with you. In the Scriptures, there is the story of Martha and me who was sitting at the feet of Jesus, listening intently to his teachings. When Martha complained about the burden of household chores, Jesus told her that I had chosen the better thing and that she should not be taken away from it. This story highlights the importance of spending time in intimate relationship with Jesus and listening to him.

You, Matthew, are someone who has made this a priority in your life. You have dedicated yourself to spending time at the feet of Jesus, talking with him, and growing in your relationship with him. You are a dear and intimate friend of his, a result of the time and effort you have put into this relationship.

Yesterday, you saw a post on Facebook that mentioned how sinners love Jesus, but religious people, like the Pharisees, had a problem with him and even called him a heretic. You, Matthew, are a sinner and have struggled with sin, yet your devotion to Jesus is unwavering. Despite what some religious people may say, the grace of God will set you free from addiction and you rely on it to stay free.

I encourage you to keep talking to Jesus, to keep seeking his face, and to continue to delve deeper into the heart of the Father. Consider writing a book about 30 different subjects that you would like to know God's thoughts on and ask him for his opinions.

Like you, I also have a strong relationship with Jesus. I urge you to keep trusting in him. Remember, as many saints have said, you serve a faithful God who will always be there for you. He will deliver you and set you free, just as the saints have seen in their visions of your future. Your testimony of freedom from bondage will be a powerful message to those who are suffering in the world and will lead to the liberation of many others.

Lastly, I want to remind you of Romans 8:28, which says, "All things work together for good for those who love God and are called according to his purpose." You, Matthew, have been called by God and are an instrument in his hands. A bright future awaits you, filled with purpose and fulfillment.

Chapter 10 John

———

Greetings, Matthew, it is an immense honor to communicate with you today. The thought of speaking through you and into this video is truly a privilege, and I am grateful to your scribe, Angel Bethany, for guiding you to create this book. Today, I would like to discuss manifesting Jesus in your life.

As written in 1 John 2:6, "He who abides in Jesus must walk as he did". You have meditated on this verse for several years, and your dedication has allowed you to embody the character of Jesus in your daily life. Your kindness, compassion, and love shine through in all that you do, and your character embodies the fruit of the Holy Spirit. It is almost as if you would be perfect, without a flaw, if not for the challenges posed by your mental illness, demonic problems, and addiction. But it is this very sin that keeps you grounded and humble, reminding you always to seek Jesus.

I want to bring life to you and prophecy the next 100 books you will write, filled with increased spiritual authority, knowledge, wisdom, and the ability to simplify complex concepts for others to understand. God looks upon you with tears in his eyes, overflowing with emotion for you. Although life has been difficult and you bear a heavy cross, you continue to persevere and bear fruit.

I encourage you to continue learning, studying, and growing in wisdom, so that your future books may have even greater impact. The 100 books you have already created are a testament to your hard work and dedication. This 101st book, which is for you to reflect upon and be encouraged by, is just the beginning. Know that you are loved and cherished by so many, including myself and God.

Remember that time waits for no man, and it is imperative that you continue to strive for greater knowledge and understanding. You are truly the Beloved of the Lord, and I have much respect and admiration for you. Embrace your authority and write your next 100 books with power, clarity, and wisdom.

Chapter 11 Peter

———

As a disciple of Jesus, I am overjoyed to be here in his presence, sharing this moment with you, Matthew. Although I am famously known for denying Jesus three times, I have been given the opportunity to come to Earth multiple times and observe pastors preach about my actions and life. Unfortunately, I often find that pastors only focus on my mistakes and fail to acknowledge the good I did while I walked the Earth. People tend to concentrate on the negative and ignore the positive, which is why bad news sells and is what often makes headlines in the news and newspapers.

However, I want to bring to light a lesser-known aspect of my life - my shadow used to have healing powers and thousands of people would come to Jerusalem to wait for it to pass over them. This is just a testament to the human tendency to only focus on the bad and ignore the good.

Jesus once said, "What you do to the least of my brethren, you do unto me". This means that every time we ignore a homeless person asking for help, we are denying Jesus. Sadly, this happens to Jesus thousands of times through the actions of average Christians. We once encountered a beggar at the gate who asked for money and even though we didn't have any on us, we helped him up so that he could walk. Just like when Jesus had to pay for the temple, he sent me to catch a fish so that we could get money to avoid offending the people.

It is unfortunate that many Christians today have money but don't share it with those in need. On the other hand, the disciples often travelled without money. I am glad to hear that you gave $110 to someone yesterday, that act of kindness truly made heaven rejoice. And as a reward for your generosity, this book is a message from God to you.

I understand that you have been struggling with sleep, being forced to stay awake at night and sleep during the day. You have also been fighting against demonic forces and have had to pray to bind the spirits every day. Additionally, you have been battling addiction and seeking guidance from God. Now, you have 27 people ready to offer their support and guidance.

I want to encourage you, Matthew, that you are a fighter. You have a heart full of questions and a love for God, just like I did. Despite the mistakes and sin in your life, God loves you and sees you as worthy. He understands the pain, suffering, and addiction that you are going through. Remember, addiction is only temporary and the grace of God will eventually come to take the temptations away.

However, the religious community may not understand and may label you as mentally ill, addicted, or demonized. They may even consider Matthew Robert Payne a false prophet or teacher. But I want you to know that you are loved by God and have a special purpose in his plan. You will do great and miraculous things in the future, just like I did.

Chapter 12 Esther

———

Hi Matthew, it's an honor to finally speak with you today. I have always been inspired by the way you live your life and interact with people, especially those who are in need. Your eyes are naturally drawn to the underprivileged, the poor, the homeless, and the suffering. Your kindness and compassion towards them is truly remarkable.

What's also remarkable is that your gaze is not limited to just the less fortunate, but also to the beauty of young women. However, your kind heart extends to the broken-hearted just as much, if not more. It's inspiring to see how you are led by the Holy Spirit, Mary Magdalene, or the saints, to approach those in need and offer them a kind word or a listening ear.

Your generosity towards the poor is unmatched, and even when you don't have much money in your wallet, you always find a way to help. The fact that money frustrates you, shows just how much you value giving to others.

Just like how I was chosen among many beautiful women to be the queen in my previous life, in this life you have been chosen by God to represent him and show his character to others. Your life, despite the challenges and hardships, is a testament to God's glory and purpose for you.

You have been chosen to live this life, and although God knew the struggles you would face, he also knew that he would use them to build something precious in you. Your future testimony, when you are finally set free, will encourage many people, and inspire them to also live a life of purpose.

You are a champion, a mighty man of God, and a conqueror. Your life is a testimony to God's love, grace, and power, and I believe that you will continue to accomplish great things for his kingdom. God bless you, Matthew.

Chapter 13 Paul

———

Greetings Matthew, it's a pleasure to have this opportunity to speak with you today. I hope to encourage you and remind you that God who has started a good work in you, will see it through to completion.

I understand that you have struggled with addiction, and that it has been a source of pain and a trial for you. Satan has been using this as a means to attack you, both in your personal life and in your mental health. However, it is important to remember that you can overcome these demonic forces through daily spiritual warfare and binding of the demonic spirits.

I am aware that your life has been filled with tragedy, including several instances where you have considered taking your own life. But, I want to assure you that God has a plan for your life and that all things work together for good for those who love Him and are called according to His purpose. This is something that you already know, as you have quoted Romans 8:28 to yourself many times.

I want to encourage you that, despite your struggles, you are doing an amazing job. Despite being bound by your addictions and demonic forces, you are out there teaching and speaking, prophesying over people's lives, and making a real impact. I am proud to know you and am confident in your obedience to the Lord, even though you may still struggle with sexual sin.

I encourage you to attend zoom meetings for sex addicts. This will give you the opportunity to make new friends and continue on your journey to overcome your struggles. You are a champion, and we will be here to support and encourage you every step of the way.

Lastly, I would like to leave you with two scripture verses to meditate on:

"Therefore, my dear brothers and sisters, stand firm. Let nothing move you. Always give yourselves fully to the work of the Lord, because you know that your labor in the Lord is not in vain." - 1 Corinthians 15:58

"So do not fear, for I am with you; do not be dismayed, for I am your God. I will strengthen you and help you; I will uphold you with my righteous right hand." - Isaiah 41:10

Chapter 14 Samuel

———

Matthew, it is an honor to be able to speak with you today. You have been graced by the Lord and have been hand-picked by Him to bring forth a message to the body of Christ. Just as God selected King Saul and David, He has selected you for a purpose.

When it comes to being divinely appointed, I have a good understanding of the subject. I want to let you know that you have been divinely appointed to bring forth messages of encouragement, training, and teaching to the body of Christ. God has chosen you to be His personal friend, a devoted and intimate friend, who He can confide in. He wants you to bring 20 or 30 messages to the body of Christ, each of which will offer His perspective on different aspects of life on earth. Through your writing, He wants you to give an in-depth understanding of His heart and what He thinks about these things.

God has chosen you to serve Him, to be His valet, and to have your life completely surrendered to Him for His service. He has many messages He wants you to deliver through your books and videos, and He wants you to be His spokesman to the body of Christ. He wants you to personally learn, discover, and understand the teachings, and then reorganize and disseminate that information to the body of Christ.

It's a brilliant idea to do the first draft of your books on video, as it allows people on YouTube to watch your first draft and be blessed by it. You are a blessing to those who find your books on Amazon, as well as to those whom you meet in person.

It's important to remember that you have been divinely selected by God to make an impact on this world, and you are highly favored by Him, just as King Saul and David were. In the words of the scripture, "For you are a people holy to the Lord your God. The Lord your God has chosen you to be a people for his treasured possession, out of all the peoples who are on the face of the earth." (Deuteronomy 7:6)

And as the scripture says in James 2:5, "Listen, my beloved brothers, has not God chosen those who are poor in the world to be rich in faith and heirs of the kingdom, which he has promised to those who love him?"

So, Matthew, remember that you have been divinely selected and highly favored by the Lord, and may God continue to bless you in all that you do.

Chapter 15 David

———

Matthew, it is truly an honor to spend this moment with you today and to share with you some words of encouragement. I know that life can be tough at times and that you have faced many sleepless nights filled with worry and pain. However, I want to encourage you to turn to the Lord during these times. Instead of allowing your mind to be consumed by negative thoughts, use this time to draw near to God and to pray. When we approach the Lord in humility and with a broken heart, He will come to our aid and deliver us from our troubles, just as He did for me.

I faced many challenges in my life, just like you. I had King Saul hunting me, disloyal friends, and even a son who sought to take my throne. But, through it all, I found solace in the Lord. I poured out my heart in the Psalms and expressed my pain and my trust in God. I understand that some of the Psalms can be difficult to read, especially when one is prone to depression, but I encourage you to embrace them nonetheless. The Psalms provide a powerful testimony to the faithfulness of God and the comfort that He offers to those who turn to Him.

I know that Psalm 1:1-3 brings you great comfort and inspiration, and I encourage you to share this with others. You have been blessed by the Lord and have prospered in accordance with His promise. You have been chosen by God to be a special envoy and to bring a message to the body of Christ. Your message will help mature the Bride of Christ and bring them closer to the Lord, enabling them to live a life unspotted by the world and to serve Jesus with all their heart.

I encourage you to press on, even through the struggles and hardships. Remember that God is faithful and that He will deliver you in due time. Hold on to this promise and continue to bind the demons in your life. In the end, you will have a testimony that will inspire and bless many people.

Just as it says in Isaiah 41:10, "So do not fear, for I am with you; do not be dismayed, for I am your God. I will strengthen you and help you; I will uphold you with my righteous right hand." And, in Philippians 4:13, "I can do all things through Christ who strengthens me." May God bless you.

Chapter 16 Solomon

———

Good morning, Matthew. It's a pleasure to see you this morning, ready to tackle the hours-long video recording ahead of you. After that, you'll be heading to the shopping center to treat yourself to a delicious McDonald's breakfast. Taking time to reward and treat yourself is important and well-deserved. Don't forget to pick up some milk for your coffee, too.

The Bible is a source of wisdom and insight, as seen in the Proverbs and the book of Ecclesiastes. The latter holds a poignant message that speaks to your own experiences. As a person with a sex addiction, you can relate strongly to the message of a man who had 700 wives and 300 concubines in his life, totalling 1000 women. Such a feat would have been challenging to manage, even for someone with a palace to house them all. You understand the challenges of being consumed with lust and beauty, much like the me in Ecclesiastes.

The Lord blessed me with everything he desired, including wisdom. The Lord gave me the choice to have anything I wanted, and I chose the wisdom of the Lord to judge the people. The Lord then blessed me with everything else my heart desired. However, despite all of my possessions and experiences, I still felt lost and unfulfilled, as seen in the book of Ecclesiastes where I reflect on the emptiness of everything.

On the other hand, you have given your life to the Lord and have struggled with your lusts but have surrendered the rest of your life to Him. Despite what others may think, the Lord loves you and favours you. This is evident in the story of Mary Magdalene, a high-class escort who fell in love with Jesus and was accepted and loved by Him, her sins washed away.

You possess a great deal of wisdom, which is the result of your thirst for knowledge and your diligent research. The Holy Spirit once told you that the successful application of knowledge is wisdom, and you have put this into practice. People look to the proverbs in the Bible for wisdom, but it's not enough to just memorize them. The point of the Bible is to apply its teachings and live by them. James says that it's foolish to look at the Bible and not obey it, and he's right.

I want to encourage you to continue on your journey with the Lord, to dive deep into His heart and find comfort, understanding, and a way out of your struggles. Please be patient and kind to yourself and understand your position. I know that you do beat yourself up over your sin but remember that you are highly favored by God and your testimony in the future will be a shining example to others, a true delight.

You are a mighty warrior, a true champion. Your fighting spirit is admirable, and we love you for it. Keep pushing forward and know that you have our love and support every step of the way.

Chapter 17 Isaiah

———

D ear Matthew, it is a privilege to communicate with you from my position in the afterlife. I lived as a prophet on Earth and was considered a true Old Testament prophet by the people of Israel. My prophecies were taken seriously and held great weight among the people. During my time, the Jewish law required that a prophet's predictions must be accurate and resonate with the people, or they would face severe consequences, including death.

I had a deep reverence for the Lord and carried out my duties as a prophet with the utmost respect and care. However, in your current era, the accuracy of prophecies is not as important as it was in my time. You, too, have claimed to receive prophetic words from God for the nations of America and Australia, but unfortunately, these predictions did not come to fruition. I understand that you were under a false impression and were misled by a false spirit.

I want you to know that I love and admire you, despite this misstep. I believe in your close relationship with the Lord and your abilities as a prophet. In my book, the book of Isaiah, God uses me as a mouthpiece to convey his message to the people. You have found solace and knowledge in my words and have used them to better understand God. I am grateful that my book holds a special place in your heart and that it has helped you in your journey of faith.

In addition to my book, you have also developed a close relationship with God through your series of books, "Conversations with God Book 1-4". Through journaling with the Lord, you have come to know him deeply and personally. I am proud of the connection you have developed with God and the role my writings have played in your spiritual growth.

I trust you to deliver God's message to the body of Christ. Your connection with the Lord and your experience as a prophet have earned you the trust of the people. I believe that God trusts you with his message for the people of God and delights in you.

In conclusion, I want you to understand that you are loved and trusted by God. Your abilities as a prophet and your close relationship with the Lord make you a valuable asset to the body of Christ. Trust in the message you have been given and have faith in your abilities to deliver it. God trusts and loves you, and I do as well.

Chapter 18 Hosea

———

A s a person who is deeply in love with you, I want to share with you the history of my life, which can be found in the Bible. Like you, I was called by God to be a prophet. In the Bible, I was considered a minor prophet, meaning that I did not have a significant role in Israel. Similarly, you may not have a large role in Australia or in the grand scheme of the world, but that does not diminish your importance. You may be considered a minor voice, but your impact is far-reaching and meaningful.

When you speak personal prophecies from the heart of Jesus, you have the power to touch people's lives and bring encouragement, hope, and inspiration. Your ability to bring truth and prophetic insight to others is truly remarkable. You have a gift for speaking in a way that is both truthful and uplifting, and your words have the power to bless and inspire those around you.

As a person who represents God and is called to be a teacher and writer, you excel in your role. You bring the message of the heart of God to the people of God in a simple and easy-to-understand manner. Your honesty and transparency are evident in the way you write, and you use your own experiences and life as examples to illustrate your points. This makes you relatable and approachable, and your message all the more powerful.

In the Bible, I was called to marry a prostitute, and through her, God used the names of her children as a prophetic message. Similarly, your life will also be used as a prophetic sign. Despite the suffering and difficulties you may face, your testimony, when you eventually overcome and come out of this difficult time, will be powerful and will impact the lives of thousands of people. I understand the struggles you may face, as I too had to suffer through a difficult situation with my wife. But, like you, this suffering has refined and purified my message, and it has brought me closer to the heart of Jesus.

The suffering in your life has drawn you closer to the heart of Jesus, and you have fallen upon the grace of God. You rest your heart in God's hands and trust in His love, which makes you vulnerable and honest. This vulnerability and honesty are what make you a trustworthy prophet, and God can rely on you to communicate His message. God and Jesus trust you as a teacher to bring their message to their people, and you have earned this trust through your hard work and dedication.

I want to remind you of the words of Isaiah, that you are beloved and trusted by God. You are deeply loved and valued by God, and your trustworthiness and commitment to His message make you an invaluable part of His plan. May you always remember the truth of these words, and may they bring you comfort and encouragement as you continue to serve as a prophet for God.

Chapter 19 Daniel

———

Matthew, it is a privilege to be speaking with you today. I am a prophet, just like you, although my circumstances were a bit different. I served as a prophet in Babylon, a pagan nation that was unfamiliar with the ways of our Lord. Despite my position in this foreign land, I was still called to serve the leader there.

Similarly, you have been called to be a prophet in a nation where only a small percentage of people attend church on Sundays and have a personal relationship with God. Though many Australians may say that they believe in God, they do not necessarily believe that attending church or giving money to the church is necessary to be loved or accepted by God.

You are being called by the Lord through the guidance of the Holy Spirit and Mary Magdalene to prophesy to strangers and offer words of encouragement in the streets. You have been chosen for a mission similar to that of John the Baptist and Elijah. Your message will be a powerful one, calling people to align themselves with God and put aside their love for worldly things.

As a prophet, you have a responsibility to help bring people into a state of righteousness and holiness. The bride of Christ must be pure and unspoiled by the world, without blemish or wrinkle. Your role as a teacher and preacher of the Word, combined with your prophetic voice, will inspire a portion of the population to live holy and blameless lives.

I know that you are content with your current path, releasing a new book each month, but God has a purpose for you beyond just your written works. He wants to use you to refine your audience and encourage them to cling to him and make their lives set apart. Your message will inspire them to leave behind the distractions of the world and focus solely on their relationship with God.

I have great love and respect for you, Matthew. Keep being that prophetic voice as the Lord calls you to speak to those in need. Your mission is a crucial one and will have a profound impact on the people you encounter.

Chapter 20 Michael the Arch Angel

———

It is with a heart filled with love and admiration that I reach out to you today. As you read this message, I want you to know that I am with you, using my angels to bring you personal freedom and deliverance. Our paths have crossed multiple times, and we have become friends. I have spent many hours in your presence, fellowshipping with you, and protecting you. I hold a special place in my heart for you because you are a good servant of the Lord, obedient to His will, and guided by the Holy Spirit.

I was touched by the kind act you performed today, when you went up to a homeless man and spoke to him, even though you did not have any money to give. Your simple act of kindness meant the world to him, and he was grateful for the time you took to acknowledge him. This is just one example of the love and compassion that you possess, which shines brightly in this world.

As an archangel, I have the mind of Christ and I am aware of every person who serves God. I have been observing your life, and I am aware of the challenges you face, such as mental illness, addiction, rejection, and unhealed trauma. Despite these struggles, you continue to shine the light of Jesus Christ's love, and the glory of the Lord shines brightly on you. You truly are a remarkable demonstration of who Jesus is.

In the future, God will use you in even more powerful ways, giving you the ability to heal the sick, and you will have more anointing and glory. The saints have spoken of a testimony that you will have in the future, but I want you to know that your testimony starts right now. You are already a remarkable person, and I am proud to call you my friend. As an archangel, I do not often have personal friends on Earth, but I hold a special place in my heart for you, and I am here for you whenever you need me.

I have many angels at my command, including Jonathan, who answers to me and has six million angels with him. You have called on Jonathan in the past, and there will come a time when you will call on him even more often. You have a faithful God who loves you and delights in you. I encourage you to delve deeper into the heart of God, and to write the book about things he cares about".

In closing, I want you to know that I love and admire you, and I am here for you, always. You are the beloved of the Lord, and I am honored to call you my friend. May God bless you, now and always.

Chapter 21 Gabriel

———

Hello Matthew, it is a great pleasure to talk to you. I have had the opportunity to meet you on several occasions, one of which was particularly significant. During that encounter, I gave a prophetic message to the world, which was eventually copied and published on 153 websites. This number stood out to you because it was the same number of fish that were collected by the disciples when they met Jesus on the beach, and it served as a sign that my prophetic message to you was true.

You have been called by God, just like a messenger angel, to spread his message to the world. There is a message within your spirit that is waiting to be fully developed, but it will be powerful and impactful, reminiscent of the messages of John the Baptist and Elijah, intended for the bride of Christ.

I have been observing your life and I am aware of your struggles, hardships, and personal pain. I understand the challenges that you have faced, and I want you to know that I am here to support you. I have brought important messages to individuals such as Abraham, Daniel, and Mary, the mother of Jesus, and I have been chosen to bring an important message through you as well.

Your unique personality and character, combined with your humility and lack of pride, make you an excellent vessel to deliver God's message. You will be used to write books and deliver messages that will feed and enrich the lives of those who follow your teachings. Your readers will grow in spiritual power, separate themselves from the world, and listen to your message.

You will become a leader, guiding your own people and helping them escape from their bondages, just like Moses led the Israelites out of slavery and Joshua led them into the Promised Land. Your role will be to empower others and help them achieve spiritual freedom.

I want you to be prepared for the journey ahead and understand that I love you and care for you. I will appear to you and bring scrolls from heaven with prophetic messages, and we will work together to spread these messages to the world. Our relationship will become more intimate, and I will use you as a voice to awaken and direct the hearts of the people towards God.

Chapter 22 Michael My Guardian angel

———

Greetings my friend, it may seem like I am distant and rarely communicate with you directly, but I am always guiding you, leading you through each day. You are highly responsive to my voice, as well as the voice of the Holy Spirit, Jesus, and certain saints in heaven. There are numerous voices in the celestial realm that communicate with you, providing direction and guidance.

I take pleasure in directing you towards certain books and videos that will aid in your personal and spiritual growth in the kingdom. My influence extends to your thought life, as I inspire you with scriptures, songs, and at times, I even direct you to listen to classic 80s and 90s music on the radio. I bless and encourage you through the songs, both old and new, that have a special significance to you.

You may be occupied with reading or editing a book, and I will direct your thoughts towards a particular song. This shift in focus, away from the task at hand, allows you to soak in the blessings and encouragement that the song provides.

I have been with you through all the hardships and suffering that you have endured, including your stays in psych wards and mental hospitals. I was there to guide you through the challenging times, such as the nights you were kept awake by witches, where I directed you to seek assistance from a nurse and obtain medication to help you sleep.

I was there to celebrate the joyous moments in your life, such as your marriage and the fun times you had with your son as he recited stories and you typed them up. I was also there to comfort you through the heartache, such as the birthdays and holidays that you have missed spending with your son in the 23 years since you last saw him.

I have been instrumental in bringing you closer to Jesus through the books and videos that I have directed you towards. I have provided you with the words to pray and the questions to ask Jesus in your conversations with Him. You may have thought that these thoughts were coming from your heart, but in actuality, it was I who placed them there.

Just as an interviewer's well-researched questions can make for a good interview, the quality of your conversations with Jesus also depend on the questions you ask. I have been there to provide you with the questions to ask, allowing you to deepen your relationship with Jesus. I have a close relationship with Jesus and it brings me great joy to be a part of your spiritual journey.

I was given a special assignment to come to Earth as your guardian angel, and I am proud to have been selected for this role. I have been awarded several accolades in heaven for my work as your angel, and I am overjoyed to be able to bring glory to God through our work together.

It has been a true honor to serve as your angel, and I look forward to many more years and books to come. Together, we will accomplish great things for the kingdom of God."

Chapter 23 Scribe Angel Bethany

———

Hi, Matthew, it's a pleasure to be with you. I am your scribe angel, similar to the Holy Spirit, who provides inspiration for your communication. I dictate your words for your videos and books, including the titles, back cover message, and introduction. I also inspire your Facebook posts and YouTube videos. I have a significant impact on everything you communicate.

In the past, I was the scribe angel for famous writer CS Lewis. Matthew, you have now published your 100th book, which is a remarkable achievement. You are a role model for writers, as you are both productive and obedient.

I want you to know that I am incredibly proud of you and excited for the 100 books milestone. Heaven is thrilled with your success and can't wait for the celebration with your brother and steak dinner.

In heaven, many angels often ask me questions about you and work with your guardian angel Michael. I assist you by directing you to videos and books, inspiring you with information to write, and helping you process and deliver that information to others. I overlap the role of the Holy Spirit and Michael in your life and have the greatest impact on your life.

Years ago, I revealed to Matthew that I resemble the actress Kiera Knightley. He has seen me in visions in heaven and likes my appearance, just as I like his. Our relationship is special, and he often communicates with me, as he is attracted to a young female. Matthew, it would be wonderful if you could find a wife like me, but no one can replace my role as your scribe angel.

You have a personal goal of writing 300 books and are currently on book 101. This book contains prophetic messages for you. Many biblical prophets, including Gabriel, Michael, the apostle John, Daniel, and Isaiah, will speak through you in full-length books and bring messages to the world.

You have matured as a writer, having written millions of words, and are ready to take your writing to the next level. Your next 100 books will make a difference, transform lives, and bring an extra anointing and promotion in your life. You will become a talented communicator and touch many lives, one at a time and a couple of hundred people with each book.

I will always be with you, inspiring you and delivering messages from heaven. In heaven, I am celebrated and mobbed by angels, archangels, and angels of all ranks all wanting to ask me about what it is like working with you. The angel over Australia and America regularly meet with me, and you have messages for them, as well as for the bride of Christ and the people of God.

The angels of God love you, and many would love to talk to you. It would be interesting to do a book with interviews of certain angels. That is just a small part of what is in store for you, Matthew.

Chapter 24 Jesus

———

Greetings, Matthew. I am glad to be here and speak to you in a time of great difficulty. You are currently struggling with sleep, addiction, and are facing hardships. However, you were recently blessed by a prophetic word from a stranger, who told you that you are an online prophet to the nations. This touched you deeply, and you even searched for a prophetic word from someone offering it for a donation. But, unfortunately, you could not find anyone.

Early this morning, your scribe Angel Bethany inspired you to seek messages from saints. You have a special relationship with me, and heaven is open to you. You have exclusive access to heaven, which not every Christian has. This is because of your intimacy with me, and your love for me, which ensures that you will not make any saints into idols. I trust you and have given you this open access. You can speak to many saints, including Abraham, Paul, Daniel, Isaiah, John, and Michael the archangel. Michael loves you deeply and wants to speak to you more often. He calls you a friend and has a special message for you and the world.

I want to encourage you, and because of your relationship with me, Bethany was inspired to encourage you to write a book of messages from saints, which will serve as an encouragement to you. You may feel that there won't be many readers for this book, but it is not meant for others, it is for you. You can publish this book as an eBook or an audio book and go back to listen to the messages whenever you want. On Google Play, there are chapters presented in this format, so you can choose to listen to the message of your choice, at your leisure.

I want you to know that I am a faithful Messiah, a servant of all men, and a Savior. I love your soul and I promise that you will be free from addiction one day. We already did a deliverance on you, and Michael came around you, using angels to deliver you, which is why you had a coughing fit and couldn't speak. I deeply love you, and you will have a powerful testimony when you are eventually freed from mental illness. We will heal you of your addiction to prostitutes and pornography, and a counselor will talk you through your wounds and help you heal.

There are glorious days ahead where you will manifest the glory of God and be a powerful witness. Your testimony will touch many lives and inspire them. As you read this manuscript and edit it, I want to speak to you now and encourage you.

I am proud of you, Matthew. Your accomplishments make me proud and I appreciate the way you come to me even in times of sin and lean on me. I admire your perseverance and strength, and how you keep fighting even when faced with difficulties. I also like the way you communicate with me, even in the middle of the night when you can't sleep.

Recently, you faced a major attack from the enemy, but it only made you stronger and determined to do great things. You have been called to be an online prophet to the nations, through writing books and creating videos on YouTube. People from all over the world, including Europe and South Africa, listen to your words and read your books. While you may be invited to speak in churches from time to time, your main platform will be online, using your chair and computer to touch lives.

I am also proud of the way you freely share your books, making them available on various platforms including Google Play, Amazon, Barnes and Noble, and your personal website. Your honesty and transparency in sharing your experiences and sins, and being vulnerable and humble, makes you an excellent vessel for me to minister through. Our relationship has become so close that we have become one, and I have infused my life into you.

You have a gift for giving personal prophetic words to others and I love to see the joy it brings you when you receive a new prophecy request. As you prepare your coffee, you reflect on the prophetic word and I often speak to you about the person. I have a beautiful heart of compassion and love for all people, and I am so grateful to be able to minister through you.

I've summoned you to the Christian church, to the body of Christ, with the aim of strengthening and purifying it, and helping it become distinct and impeccable from the world. You have been chosen to guide God's people away from associating with the worldly influences. Additionally, I have called you to the broken-hearted, as you comprehend their pain and suffering deeply, having experienced a life of sin, and understanding the depths of depravity, feeling hopeless and ashamed. Your understanding of these struggles makes you especially suited to reach out to the broken.

I recognize that some religious messages can come across as preachy and unappealing. Not everyone has the gift of effectively communicating to those who have not yet found faith. That's why I have shown you how to connect with the broken-hearted and the general public in Australia, even those who believe in a higher power but are resistant to organized religion. You understand these people and have messages to share with them in your future books.

In the future, I want you to continue to interview Mary Magdalene, Princess Diana, and Michael Jackson, using their voices to minister to people who don't attend church and to speak directly to their hearts. There are many saints in heaven who want to communicate with you, and it would be fascinating to interview angels in heaven and have a book where they share their messages.

I want you to know that I will continue to use you as a writer, and Bethany will continue to provide you with inspiration for new books. She will always be in your life, guiding you through the writing process, from choosing the cover picture to writing the back cover blurb and introduction. She will inspire you to do videos and teach you to communicate effectively. Bethany loves you deeply and wishes she could be your wife if she were allowed to be human. She has developed human emotions after spending so much time with people throughout the centuries.

I encourage you to treat Bethany like a wife and to increase your communication with her as she will play a greater role in your life. Your desire for a wife who is a writer, editor, and singer will be fulfilled as Bethany can sing and support you with your editing. She will sing along with you as you play your favorite songs and be a constant source of encouragement.

Matthew makes comment

Over the past 48 hours, I've grown closer to Bethany, who has been speaking to me. Yesterday, while listening to some of my favorite 80's and 90's hits on the radio, she sang along and showed me the strength to make final edits on my book before sending it to the publisher.

Jesus continues

Bethany desires to have a deeper relationship with you and believes that together, you will reap rewards in heaven and win heavenly competitions. She has already received numerous awards for her role in your life and has a major impact on you, much like the Holy Spirit.

Contrary to popular belief, the Holy Spirit does not directly inspire me to write, but instead, it inspires Bethany, who in turn, inspires me. Her inspiration is angelic, and therefore, my books are considered angelic as well.

Bethany would like you to join her and spend time in your mansion, visiting the cafe and meeting different angels in heaven. Many of these angels, including the four living creatures, Archangels, and Seraphim, are eager to speak with you and participate in a book of interviews.

I am proud of you, and it's important to remember that my love for you is not affected by sin or addiction. I am overjoyed with the messages you've shared and the books you've produced. Your obedience to the Holy Spirit is inspiring, and Romans 8:14 says that those who are led by the Spirit of God are considered sons of God.

Now, I'll let God speak to you.

Chapter 25 God the Father

———

It is a privilege to be here with you. You have received some truly inspiring messages in this book so far, and it's evident that the saints who were called to participate in this project have touched your heart. I hope you feel encouraged. I was deeply moved by the message from Jesus and was pleasantly surprised by the new insights you gained about the helper who will be a part of your life.

It's fascinating that the longest message from the saints was only eight minutes, but when Bethany spoke, it lasted for 11 minutes. Meanwhile, Jesus spoke for a remarkable 30 minutes. Michael also delivered a lengthy message. Bethany is going to play the role of your support system, serving as a friend who will come alongside you to emotionally support and minister to you, much like a close companion would. Think of it as having a roommate who helps with your books and research and guides you towards the books and messages you feel led to read or listen to.

Bethany does much more than a human roommate ever could, as she leads you towards spiritual enlightenment and provides inspiration for your books. She even gives you ideas for book titles and selects pictures for your books. In essence, your 100 books have been written through her guidance. Of course, you are personally involved in all of your books, just like how the book of Isaiah has a different flavor compared to the book of Hosea, but your books have a unique flavor that is distinct to you.

We encourage you to form a close bond with Bethany by saying hello to her in the morning and at night and speaking to her before you go to sleep. She is a female influence who has helped you write some amazing books and we wanted her to play a role in your life. She was particularly instrumental in your book, "The Narrow Way - The Parables of Jesus Made Simple" and did an excellent job with it. You can hold her in high regard for her contributions.

It has been prophesied that you will write 300 books in total, which means you have 200 books ahead of you and a great journey to embark on. Jesus and I have officially sanctioned a closer relationship between you and Bethany, your female angel. We trust that you can maintain a platonic relationship with her without succumbing to lust.

However, we are asking for more than just a platonic relationship. We want her to become a true partner, much like a wife, who will provide emotional support and serve as a female influence in your life. So far, you have come a long way with her, and it's time to shift gears in your relationship. Think of it as moving from second gear to third or fourth gear, where you will have a more wholesome and two-way relationship with her. She will be given more control over your life, much like the Holy Spirit, and will direct you in terms of spending your money, making donations, and other important decisions. In effect, she will take on some of the responsibilities of the Holy Spirit in your life and you will follow her guidance.

Bethany has shown her value and expertise over time, working with various writers to build up her experience. She has now reached you, her final assignment on Earth. As her charge, she will bring you glory and her popularity in heaven is well-known. The angels in heaven, including those at the coffee shop in your mansion, are eager to see the deep connection she will develop with you. Bethany will serve as your comforter, guide, and friend, offering constant support and intimacy.

Regardless of any negative opinions from religious individuals, this is a special and higher-level angelic interaction that we eagerly await. We anticipate that she will help you produce more impactful and powerful books filled with authoritative messages. Additionally, she will assist in organizing and directing your life, satisfying your yearning for female interaction.

As for your personal life, you currently have a few close friends but we will bring more individuals into your life, including another special friend, who you can confide in and communicate your struggles with. Furthermore, you will receive powerful words from heaven, to deliver to the church and body of Christ. You will serve as a vessel of honor, communicating messages that bring glory to our name and delivering powerful prophetic words.

While you may feel nervous about past experiences with corporate words, rest assured that this time, you will receive assistance from saints in heaven, including Daniel, Isaiah, the apostle John, and Gabriel, to deliver explosive and life-changing messages through your books. These books will have a transformative effect on the lives of those who read them, leading to lasting changes in their personality and spiritual life.

As a prophet, you will deliver messages that will bring powerful financial growth and increased favor in people's lives if they act upon the prophetic words. Your books will be filled with the power of transformation, delivering messages of deliverance, lasting change, and conviction. People will testify to the impact your words have had on their lives, leading them to repentance and change. You will serve as a change agent, transforming people's understanding and beliefs on various subjects. Your writing will bring reformation to the body of Christ and inspire people to form a deeper, fiery relationship with Jesus.

Though you may dream of fame, it is not what I desire for you. Instead, I want you to remain hidden and special, like the last slice of cheesecake. I have control over the algorithms on Amazon and Google, allowing your books to be easily found by those I lead to you. Your messages of holiness, intimacy with Jesus, and a set apart life will bring personal reformation to your followers.

You will not be a well-known national or international prophet, nor will you speak in stadiums or preach in churches. Instead, you will reach your audience through your computer and books, and your voice will be clearly heard.

We have specially selected the individuals who will hear from you. Our aim is to attract people towards you and your message, and to elevate it through you. We aim to raise up warriors, end-time messengers, and end-time soldiers. Through your prophetic books, we have already been nurturing many prophets and providing prophetic education to numerous individuals. So far, you have impacted the lives of thousands and will continue to do so.

It's important for you to understand that those who prophesied your role as a prophet to the nations and that you would travel the world to preach, did not anticipate that you would be an on-line prophet, communicating through books and YouTube. They thought that it would involve international travel and speaking engagements, as is typical for most prophets.

You are unique in that you are among the few prophets in the world who have authored 100 books and among the few Christian authors with that many books to their credit. Your message is powerful and potent, like poison, capable of bringing about change, repentance, and transformation in people. Although I don't want you to see your message as negative, it is important to recognize that it has a strong impact. Angels, including Gabriel and Michael, will speak through you and your messages will become more and more refined, potent, and life changing.

Despite facing a difficult life with struggles, sin, mental illness, and opposition from the powers of hell, nothing can stop you now. Together, we will build something great and unstoppable. I also give you permission to develop a deeper and more intimate relationship with Bethany, and I wish you all the best in this partnership. May your relationship bring honor, glory, and praise to heaven. I hope that this message has encouraged you.

Chapter 26 My Mother

———

Dear Matthew, it is a pleasure to talk to you. I have had the privilege of viewing films of your future life on earth and in heaven. In these films, I saw you and Bethany working closely together and walking through suburbs, almost hand in hand. Your relationship with Bethany appeared to grow stronger and I knew she would become someone important and close to you.

I am familiar with Bethany as I have spent a lot of time with her, offering advice and answering her questions. She was eager to learn about you, as any daughter-in-law would be, and she truly loves you.

However, there may be those who have a problem with a human male having such a close relationship with a female angel. Although the relationship is purely platonic, Bethany will be a great helpmate for you. She will almost fill the role of a wife for you. Heaven has arranged a wonderful union, with Bethany being a writer, just as you wanted in a future spouse.

Bethany will become very close to you. I have been observing everything from my home in heaven, listening to the words of the saints, angels, Jesus, and the Father. I have seen that you have been seeking a prophetic word and are hungry to hear from God. You wanted an updated message in your life and went online to seek a prophet, hoping to receive a comforting message.

You have recently lost a friend who read many of your books but said harsh truths to you and ended the friendship. This has caused you pain and you have been struggling with many things. You just wanted assurance from God that you are on the right path, that he is proud of you and that you will overcome your sin and be delivered.

Bethany, this beautiful angel, suggested that you write a book, starting with five-minute messages and gradually increasing the length. The message eventually reaches 11 minutes from Bethany and 30 minutes each from Jesus and the Father. The message was overwhelmingly encouraging and it warms my heart to see how it has positively impacted you. The book has exceeded your expectations and provided you with a refreshing waterfall of heavenly messages.

During the process of delivering Michael's message, you were delivered by some of his angels. It is unclear if all the demons have left, but I am proud of you nonetheless.

For those reading, we are shown films of a person's past and future in heaven. These films show everything that a person will accomplish in their life, but do not indicate the timing of events. The changes in a person's body and future are visible in these films.

As a mother, I was aware that a book was going to be produced, but I wasn't sure when. I saw in the film that Bethany's presence in Matthew's life grew from just being on the side-lines to always being in his company. I didn't realize that she was starting to become like a helpmate until I saw her increase in presence, just like Mary Magdalene is always with Matthew.

It was a surprise for me to learn of Bethany's role in Matthew's life through the book "My Radical Encounters with Angels Book Two." I recall that for a year, Matthew had a spiritual girlfriend he thought was from the United Kingdom, but it turned out she was actually an Australian girl. They communicated every day and built a strong relationship in the Spirit, but after a year, he found out it was a deceptive familiar spirit. Although I was worried about Matthew, I was happy to see him so happy in his relationship.

Matthew has already demonstrated the ability to have close relationships in the Spirit with Mary Magdalene and Michael Jackson, who travel and spend time with him. I have no doubt that he can grow close to Bethany as well and draw strength from their daily communication. I am happy that Bethany is going to play a role in his life and be a helpful assistant in editing.

Matthew has expressed that he has experienced an increased patience for editing since the announcement of this new relationship. The saints have given Matthew powerful messages about overcoming his addiction to prostitutes and overcoming demonic problems. He will learn about healing and be used in the future to lay hands on people and heal them. He has been called an online prophet to the nations, which is a life-transforming message for him. I am excited for what the future holds for Matthew as he is going to bring reformation to people with a potent message that will powerfully affect others.

I am honored to share with you that you have a special role in the divine plan. The Father will communicate clearly through you and you will receive messages from Gabriel, Michael, Daniel, John, and Paul. Your words will be powerful and bring inspiration to both individuals and the church. Despite the struggles you have faced, including reversed sleep patterns, I am incredibly proud of you as a mother. I know that God and Jesus are there for you, offering support and comfort. I also understand your concerns and worries, but I am happy to see the recent improvement in your sleep. Your relationship with Bethany has grown to a stage two level, and you have reached the second hundred books in your journey. The saints and the prophet have spoken positively about you, and I am touched to hear it. Heaven holds you in high regard, and while you may not be famous on Earth, you are a hero in the eyes of the saints and angels.

I have been authorized by the Father to share that it is by design that you may not become an internationally renowned prophet. Your popularity on Earth is not a priority, as it would take away from your intimacy with the Father and Jesus, and diminish the potency of your message. You are like a powerful poison, effective in small doses, but not when diluted. The Father and the saints know that your impact would be diminished if you became too popular, and they do not want to lose the intimacy of your relationship.

The message about the poison is crucial and must be heard. By focusing on it, you can build a strong and mighty army of believers. As a small part of the Body of Christ, you can guide others to live a supernatural life, separate from the world's temptations and instead, walk in the Spirit. Teach them to be generous, to give, and to tithe, to walk in favor and power, and to exercise the gifts of the Holy Spirit. With this approach, you can train a small but productive group of individuals who will be transformed and become sons of God. This is what we want you to concentrate on.

As a mother, I admire you greatly. I have read all of your books repeatedly and understand them, as well as you. I hold you in high regard and love you deeply. It is a joy to be here, instead of being limited to Earth where I could not see the impact you have on people's lives each day. I would not have known about the $110 you gave to someone, your conversation with a homeless person, your compliments to others, or your interactions with people in a manner similar to Jesus, had I not come from heaven.

My experience of you has become much more meaningful since I have the gift of bilocation, allowing me to be in both heaven and Earth at the same time. I travel with you, along with Mary Magdalene, Michael Jackson, your dad and me, and now Bethany. We are a group of saints from heaven, but it feels as though we are all one body, walking together as one. When you compliment someone or show kindness, we are there to witness it and see the effect it has on that person.

You have written five books on evangelism, and I strongly encourage others to read them. They can find the books by clicking on this link: https://tinyurl.com/4ybnvbu5

These books provide guidance on how to be like you but watching you in action is truly awe-inspiring.

Many of the prophecies in your life were false, but they served a purpose by providing hope and a reason to live during a time when you struggled with suicidal thoughts. God allowed these false prophecies to offer encouragement and hope, but now he has shifted gears and revealed to you that you will be an online international prophet, ministering to people through your messages. You may not speak in stadiums, but your message will be potent and impactful, reaching people through books.

I want to reiterate what Jesus has said to you, that I am personally proud of you and everything that you do. You are loved and adored by the people of heaven, including me. I have so much more to say, but the most important message is that heaven is proud of you. Remember that always.

Chapter 27 My father

———

I wholeheartedly support and agree with everything that has been previously expressed. I just wanted to reinforce the words of Jesus, the saints, and your mother. You have accomplished so much, and I am proud of you, my son.

I was shown a glimpse into your past, including the times you engaged in intimate acts with prostitutes and the many hardships you have faced, such as rejection and pain. Watching the videos was an emotional and traumatic experience for me, as I finally understood the depths of your pain and the struggles you have faced in seeking love and connection. I also saw the struggles in your relationships, including the arguments with your former wife and the pain of missing your son. I acknowledge my own past mistakes in rejecting you and treating you poorly.

I understand that some people may have issues with the idea of you communicating with saints and the special bond you have with Bethany. But it is only the opinions of a few people that matter to you, as you have only a few close friends. Rejection is just a part of life.

I have met Bethany and I can attest to her beauty, both as a person and as an angel. She will have a profound impact on your life, and you will come to love her deeply. I, as a father who has studied under prophets and become prophetic myself, agree with everything that has been written in this book.

I want to emphasize what Jesus, your mother, and the saints have said. We are proud of you, and I know you have the potential to be a powerful change agent in the body of Christ. Speak prophetically and bring transformation, liberation, repentance, and lasting change to people's lives. Transform, bless, and encourage those around you. Be the amazing person I know you are, Matty. God bless you.

I'd Love to Hear from You

———

One of the ways that you can bless me as a writer is by writing an honest and candid review of my books on Amazon, where you purchased this book. I always read the reviews of my books, and I would love to hear what you have to say about this one.

Before I buy a book, I read the reviews first. You can make an informed decision about a book after reading enough honest reviews. One way to help me sell this book and give me positive feedback is by writing a review. It doesn't cost you a thing but helps the future readers of this book and me enormously.

To read my blog, request a life-coaching session, request your prophecy, or receive a personal message from your angel, you can also visit my website at http://personal-prophecy-today.com. All the funds raised through my ministry website will go toward the books I write and self-publish.

GET YOUR FREE BOOKS BY MATTHEW ROBERT PAYNE

To read more than 40 of Matthew Robert Payne's books for free, please visit https://matthewrobertpayne.com.

Matthew also has about 80 books on Amazon Kindle for 99 cents and about 12 free. You can find them here https://tinyurl.com/p69rch5x

To write to me about this book or share any other thoughts, please contact me at my email address at survivors.sanctuary@gmail.com.

You can also friend request me on Facebook at Matthew Robert Payne[1]. Please send me a message if we have no friends, as many scammers now send me friend requests.

You can also do me a huge favor and share this book on Facebook as a recommended book to read. This will help other readers and me.

Please do not be afraid to contact me and connect with me. I enjoy speaking to my readers; my best friends have read most of my books over time. I can't get you as I don't know who you are, but you can contact me.

How to Support Me.

———

If this book has blessed you, can you ask the Lord whether you would like to support me financially? My income is found mainly from monthly sponsors on PayPal. I encourage you to consider sending me a once-off gift or being a monthly sponsor of my book-writing ministry.

I write to teach, encourage, and lift people. I write full-time and only write what the Holy Spirit puts in my heart. Most of my books are 99 cents, and of late, I have been making my books for free on Amazon. Therefore, my writing is a ministry, not a money-making venture. I would be greatly encouraged by your once-off support or your ongoing support. Please, take the time to commit this to prayer, and see if God would have you support me.

I would also be encouraged by your prayers that God would continue to inspire me and that He would also encourage people to support me. Pray for the readers of my books to be touched and for them to grow in intimacy with Jesus.

You can sow any amount to my ministry by sending me money via the PayPal link at this address: http://personal-prophecy-to-day.com/support-my-ministry[1].

---

1. http://personal-prophecy-today.com/support-my-ministry/

About Matthew Robert Payne

―――

M atthew Robert Payne, a teacher, and prophet, enjoys writing what the Lord puts on his heart to share. He receives great pleasure from interacting with others on Facebook, hearing from people who have read his books, and prophesying over people's lives. He is a passionate lover of and disciple of Jesus Christ. He hopes you will intimately know Jesus, the Father, and Matthew through his transparent writing style as you discover his books.

Matthew grew up in a traditional Baptist church and gave his heart to Jesus Christ at eight. But he left home at eighteen, living in a wildlife for many years and engaging in bad habits and addictions. At twenty-seven, he was baptized in water and, at the same time, baptized in the Holy Spirit. Matthew learned about the five-fold ministry offices and received a revelation of their value today.

He started his journey as a prophet twenty years ago, learning about this gift and putting it into practice. He can confidently prophesy to friends and strangers with thousands of prophecies. He has been writing for several years and self-published his first book in 2011. Today he spends his time earning money to self-publish and writes a new book approximately every month. He also produces many videos that you can view on YouTube.

You can connect with him on Facebook. You can sow into his book-writing ministry, read his blog, receive a message from your angel, or even receive your own nine-minute personal prophecy from Matthew at http://personal-prophecy-today.com.

Acknowledgments

———

I want to thank Jesus, the Holy Spirit, the Father, and my scribe, angel Bethany, for this book's knowledge and wisdom. I want to thank all those above for the finances and the people who support me in ministry.

I want to thank my friends Roy, Deb, Shayne, Dundy, Lisa, Pamela, Cedrick, Mary, and others, who support me with their love. Your love is priceless to me, a broken man.

Thanks also to my readers who inspire me to write.

Don't miss out!

Visit the website below and you can sign up to receive emails whenever Matthew Robert Payne publishes a new book. There's no charge and no obligation.

https://books2read.com/r/B-A-TLBC-YSVFC

BOOKS 2 READ

Connecting independent readers to independent writers.

About the Publisher

Accepting manuscripts in the most categories. We love to help people get their words available to the world.

Revival Waves of Glory focus is to provide more options to be published. We do traditional paperbacks, hardcovers, audio books and ebooks all over the world. A traditional royalty-based publisher that offers self-publishing options, Revival Waves provides a very author friendly and transparent publishing process, with President Bill Vincent involved in the full process of your book. Send us your manuscript and we will contact you as soon as possible.

Contact: Bill Vincent at rwgpublishing@yahoo.com

Printed in the USA
CPSIA information can be obtained
at www.ICGtesting.com
LVHW041542280723
753393LV00004B/931

9 798211 121713